WILD RIDES

Planes

An Hachette UK Company
www.hachette.co.uk

First published in Great Britain in 2012 by
TickTock, a division of Octopus Publishing Group Ltd
Endeavour House
189 Shaftesbury Avenue
London
WC2H 8JY
www.octopusbooks.co.uk

ISBN 978 1 84898 635 0

A CIP catalogue record for this book is available from the British Library

Printed and bound in China

10 9 8 7 6 5 4 3 2 1

Picture credits:
b=bottom; c=center; t=top; r=right; l=left
Aviation Picture Library: p.1, p.6-7, p.10-11, p.16-17, p.18-19, p.20-21, p.30-31. Corbis: p.4-5, p.26-27. iStockphoto.com: p.8-9. Lockheed: p.22-23. NASA: p.12-13, p.24-25, p.28-29. Skyscan: p.14-15.

Every effort has been made to trace the copyright holders, and we apologise in advance for any unintentional omissions. We would be pleased to insert the appropriate acknowledgments in any subsequent edition of this publication.

Contents

Ever since the first plane took to the skies, aircraft have become bigger and bigger. In 2007, European manufacturer Airbus introduced the largest commercial aircraft to date: the enormous Airbus A380.

This gentle giant is the quietest wide-body jetliner in the air. It generates 50 per cent less noise than its nearest competitor.

DID YOU KNOW?
During take-off the wings of the A380 flex upward by over 4 metres.

The double-decker A380 can carry up to 853 passengers.

The A380 includes open spaces and social areas. The interiors can be custom-designed. Singapore Airlines' A380s include separate sitting and sleeping areas, complete with full-sized beds!

LAUNCHED: 2007

ORIGIN: EUROPE (SPECIFICALLY FRANCE, GERMANY, SPAIN AND THE UK)

MODELS: A380-800 PASSENGER PLANE; A380-800F FOR CARGO

ENGINES: TWO NEW-GENERATION ENGINE OPTIONS: THE ENGINE ALLIANCE GP7200 AND ROLLS-ROYCE TRENT 900

WINGSPAN: 79.8 M

LENGTH: 72.75 M

COCKPIT CREW: TWO

SEATING: UP TO 853

MAXIMUM SPEED: 945 KM/H (588 MPH)

MAXIMUM WEIGHT: 569 TONNES FOR TAKE-OFF

RANGE: 14,800 KM (9,200 MILES)

LOAD: UP TO 853 PASSENGERS OR 150 TONNES OF CARGO

COST: ABOUT £155 MILLION

SR-71 Blackbird

In 1960, the Soviet Union shot down an American spy plane. After this disaster the US government hired Lockheed Corporation to build a craft that would never be shot down. The result was the amazing SR-71, packed with cameras and sensors. Despite its dangerous missions, not one of the 32 Blackbirds built was lost in combat.

Nicknamed 'Blackbird' because of its dark color, the plane is made of titanium alloy, which protects it from the extreme heat produced by flying at Mach 3.

DID YOU KNOW?

The SR-71 flight manual contains over 1,000 pages and is available online.

The Blackbird was top secret. President Lyndon Johnson didn't even admit it existed until six months after its maiden flight in 1964.

WARNING
Restricted Area

Large spikes keep the plane balanced.

STATS & FACTS

LAUNCHED: 1966

RETIRED: 1998

ORIGIN: US

MODELS: SR-71A, SR-71B; OTHER VARIANTS INCLUDE THE A-12, YF-12A, M-21 AND D-21 DRONE

ENGINES: TWO PRATT & WHITNEY J58-P-10S WITH AFTERBURNERS

WINGSPAN: 16.94 M

LENGTH: 31.65 M

COCKPIT CREW: TWO

MAXIMUM SPEED: MACH 3 (3,500 KM/H / 2,200 MPH)

MAXIMUM WEIGHT: 64 TONNES

RANGE: 5,400 KM (3,300 MILES)

LOAD: SENSORS AND CAMERAS

COST: £33 MILLION TO BUILD; £30,000 AN HOUR TO FLY

The 787 Dreamliner is the first mid-sized commercial aircraft able to fly long-range routes. In service since 2011, the Dreamliner incorporates breatkthrough technologies that make it 20 per cent more fuel efficient than airplanes of the same size.

The 787 has a smooth nose shape.

DID YOU KNOW?

The 787 is equipped with systems that report its maintenance requirements directly to ground-based computers.

The larger 787-9 can carry up to 290 passengers on routes of 15,750 km (9,450 miles).

The four-panel windscreen and large windows offer a good view of the horizon.

STATS & FACTS

LAUNCHED: 2004

ORIGIN: US

MODELS: 787-8, 787-9

ENGINES: TWO GENERAL ELECTRIC OR ROLLS ROYCE ENGINES

WINGSPAN: 60 M

LENGTH: UP TO 63 M

COCKPIT CREW: TWO

CRUISING SPEED: MACH 0.85 (1,041 KM/H / 647 MPH)

MAXIMUM TAKE-OFF WEIGHT: 247 TONNES

RANGE: 15,750 KM (9,800 MILES)

LOAD: UP TO 290 PASSENGERS

COST: £119 TO 140 MILLION

The cabin windows on the 787 are the largest of any commercial aircraft and use 'smart glass' that dims automatically. No shutters are needed!

B-2 Spirit

Stealth airplanes are designed to avoid detection by enemy radar. First flown in 1989, the B-2 stealth bomber looks like it came from another planet.

B-2 technology comes at a price – each plane costs an amazing £716 million!

The strange bulges in the B-2 hide its engines, cockpit and bombs.

DID YOU KNOW?

The B-2's skin is jet-black and smooth and all joints are hidden.

The plane has just two crew members: a pilot and a mission commander. The rest of the cockpit contains computer-controlled flight equipment.

STATS & FACTS

LAUNCHED: 1989

ORIGIN: US

MODELS: THE US AIR FORCE HAS 20 PLANES, ALL SLIGHTLY DIFFERENT

ENGINES: FOUR GENERAL ELECTRIC F118-GE-100 ENGINES, EACH WITH A THRUST OF 7,850 KG

WINGSPAN: 52 M

LENGTH: 21 M

COCKPIT CREW: TWO

MAXIMUM SPEED: HIGH SUBSONIC

MAXIMUM WEIGHT: 181 TONNES

RANGE: INTERCONTINENTAL

LOAD: CONVENTIONAL OR NUCLEAR WEAPONS

COST: £716 MILLION

B-52 Stratofortress

After World War II, the US Air Force built B-52s – monster eight-engined jet bombers. In 1952, the first of these giants took flight. Still flying and fighting, they will be in service until at least 2040. Today's pilots say that the last B-52 pilot has not yet been born.

Fighter pilots refer to the B-52 as 'BUFF': Big Ugly Fat Fellow.

Sensors enable the plane to fly close to the ground during combat missions.

DID YOU KNOW?

The B-52 has six ejection seats.

Air refuelling makes it possible for B-52s to fly almost anywhere in the world.

STATS & FACTS

LAUNCHED: 1952

ORIGIN: US

MODELS: B-52A TO B-52H

ENGINES: EIGHT PRATT & WHITNEY TF-33 TURBOFAN ENGINES

WINGSPAN: 56.4 M

LENGTH: 49 M

COCKPIT CREW: SIX

MAXIMUM SPEED: 1,046 KM/H (650 MPH)

MAXIMUM WEIGHT: 221 TONNES

RANGE: 14,160 KM (8,800 MILES)

LOAD: NUCLEAR OR HIGH-EXPLOSIVE BOMBS, CRUISE MISSILES AND A VARIETY OF GUNS

COST: £6 MILLION (IN 1952)

Concorde

In 1962, Britain and France joined forces to build a supersonic commercial aircraft – *Concorde*.

First flown in 1969, *Concorde* entered service in 1976 and flew for 27 years before being retired.

Cruising at Mach 2 – twice the speed of sound – this amazing plane made the trip from London to New York in just over three hours.

Concorde's slim body and paper-dart shape enabled it to fly more than twice as fast as other passenger planes.

DID YOU KNOW?

Twenty *Concordes* were built. Five are now on show in museums.

Concorde's entire nose hinged down so the pilot could see when landing.

Concorde's four powerful engines allowed the plane to reach 363 km/h (225 mph) in just 30 seconds.

STATS & FACTS

LAUNCHED: 1977

ORIGIN: FRANCE AND THE UK

MODELS: ONLY ONE PRODUCTION TYPE, WHICH IS LARGER THAN PROTOTYPES

ENGINES: FOUR ROLLS-ROYCE/ SNECMA OLYMPUS S93 TURBOJETS, PROVIDING 17,260 KG THRUST

WINGSPAN: 25.6 M

LENGTH: 61.66 M

COCKPIT CREW: TWO PILOTS

MAXIMUM SPEED: MACH 2 (2,173 KM/H / 1,350 MPH)

MAXIMUM WEIGHT: 185 TONNES

RANGE: 7,242 KM (4,500 MILES)

LOAD: ROOM FOR 140 PASSENGERS, BUT USUALLY SEATED 100

COST: £23 MILLION (IN 1977); THIS WOULD BE ABOUT £200 MILLION TODAY

Eurofighter Typhoon

Four European countries – Germany, Italy, Spain and the UK – developed this warplane together. Typhoons are built on four separate assembly lines, with each country building its own national aircraft.

Only 15 per cent of the Eurofighter's body is metal. The rest is mainly lightweight carbon fibre, which keeps the plane from overheating.

DID YOU KNOW?

By January 2011, Typhoons in service since 2003 had flown over 100,000 hours.

The twin engines allow the Typhoon to accelerate to Mach 1 – the speed of sound – in under 30 seconds. The Typhoon also takes off in just 5 seconds!

The Typhoon has a large triangular wing and small powered foreplanes on each side of the nose.

LAUNCHED: 2002

ORIGIN: EUROPE

MODELS: TWIN-ENGINE, CANARD-DELTA WING MULTIROLE AIRCRAFT ENGINES: TWO EUROJET EJ200 REHEATED TURBOFANS EACH PROVIDING 9,072 KG THRUST

WINGSPAN: 10.95 M

LENGTH: 15.96 M

COCKPIT CREW: ONE OR TWO

MAXIMUM SPEED: MACH 2 (2,495 KM/H / 1,550 MPH)

MAXIMUM WEIGHT: 23.5 TONNES

RANGE: 2,900 KM (1,800 MILES)

LOAD: GUNS, MISSILES, BOMBS

COST: £65 MILLION

F-117A Nighthawk

First flown in 1981, the F-117A could be the weirdest aircraft ever made. Its shape was designed to break up enemy radar signals. Because it could be refuelled in midair, the F-117A was able to fly almost anywhere. Retired in 2008, this amazing plane was made by the US company Lockheed.

Three Nighthawks are on display in the US. At the United States Air Force Museum visitors can walk right up to this incredible aircraft.

DID YOU KNOW?

Nighthawk pilots called themselves 'Bandits'.

The F-117A was a bomber plane. Its zigzag-shaped doors opened and shut very quickly to release bombs.

The hundreds of flat surfaces on the plane made it almost invisible on radar.

STATS & FACTS

LAUNCHED: 1981

RETIRED: 2008

ORIGIN: US

MODELS: FIVE PROTOTYPES AND 59 PRODUCTION AIRCRAFT

ENGINES: TWO GENERAL ELECTRIC F404-F1D2 TURBOFANS, EACH GIVING 4,899 KG THRUST

WINGSPAN: 13.2 M

LENGTH: 20.08 M

COCKPIT CREW: ONE

MAXIMUM SPEED: MACH 1 (993 KM/H / 617 MPH)

MAXIMUM WEIGHT: 23.4 TONNES

RANGE: WITHOUT AIR REFUELLING, ABOUT 2,400 KM (1,500 MILES)

LOAD: TWO LASER-GUIDED BOMBS

COST: £23.6 MILLION

Harrier

By the late 1950s, air forces wanted planes that could operate from car parks, forest clearings, or even small ships. Hawker Aircraft in the UK launched one of the first VTOL (Vertical Take-off and Landing) aircraft in 1969. This plane is the Harrier. It is also known as the 'Jump Jet'.

DID YOU KNOW?

The US Marine Corps uses the Harrier to provide air power for forces invading an enemy shore.

This single-seat Sea Harrier operates from aircraft carriers. There are also two-seater and training versions.

Harriers have a system called VIFF (Vectoring in Forward Flight) that lets them perform tricky manoeuvres.

STATS & FACTS

LAUNCHED: 1969

ORIGIN: UK

MODELS: ELEVEN VERSIONS

ENGINES: ONE ROLLS-ROYCE PEGASUS 6 OR 11, DEPENDING ON THE VERSION; THE VECTORED THRUST TURBOFAN PROVIDES 6,800 KG TO 10,660 KG THRUST, DEPENDING ON THE VERSION

WINGSPAN: UP TO 9.25 M

LENGTH: UP TO 14.5 M

COCKPIT CREW: ONE TO TWO

MAXIMUM SPEED: MACH 1 (1,180 KM/H / 735 MPH)

MAXIMUM WEIGHT: UP TO 14 TONNES

RANGE: WITHOUT AIR REFUELLING, ABOUT 2,736 KM (1,700 MILES)

LOAD: MISSILES, ROCKETS, BOMBS

COST: £14.5 TO 18.5 MILLION

The engine has two nozzles on each side. They blast downward for take-off and forward to slow down.

Joint Strike Fighter

In 1995, the US Air Force and US Navy launched a program for a JSF (Joint Strike Fighter). The goal was to produce the next generation of planes for airfields and aircraft carriers.

All JSFs carry weapons on each side of the fuselage.

DID YOU KNOW?

The JSF will replace fighter, strike and ground attack aircraft for the US, UK, Canada, Australia, and their allies.

There are three versions of the JSF. The F-35A is the basic version. The F-35B has a more powerful engine. The F-35C (right) has a bigger wing, which can fold.

The rear exhaust produces thrust to lift the aircraft.

STATS & FACTS

LAUNCHED: 1995

ORIGIN: US

MODELS: F-35A, F-35B, AND F-35C

ENGINES: ONE PRATT & WHITNEY F135 TURBOFAN OR ONE F136 GE TURBOFAN; FOR THE F-35B, ONE F135 PRATT & WHITNEY TURBOFAN OR ONE F136 GE TURBOFAN AND ROLLS-ROYCE ALLISON ENGINE-DRIVEN LIFT FAN, DELIVERING 11, 340 KG AND 8,164 KG THRUST

WINGSPAN: UP TO 13.1 M

LENGTH: UP TO 15.5 M

COCKPIT CREW: ONE

MAXIMUM SPEED: MACH 1.8 (1,900 KM/H / 1,200 MPH)

MAXIMUM WEIGHT: 22.7 TONNES

RANGE: ABOUT 2,200 KM (1,380 MILES)

LOAD: ENORMOUS VARIETY OF GUNS, MISSILES AND BOMBS

COST: £57 MILLION

Space Shuttle

Early space flights relied on rockets – giant tubes fired into orbit. The Space Shuttle was the first spacecraft that could be brought back to Earth. NASA used it on 135 missions from 1981 to 2011, when it was retired.

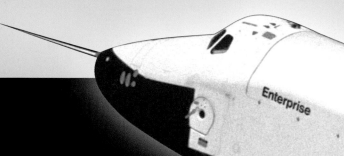

The front area houses 10 crew members, including two pilots. In the middle is a large bay for satellites. At the back are three big rocket engines.

DID YOU KNOW?

The Shuttle's boosters fall off into the ocean. They are recovered and used again.

Heat-resistant tiles protect the Shuttle when it returns to Earth. It glides onto a runway and is slowed down by a big parachute.

The orbiter is attached to a huge tank holding liquid oxygen and liquid hydrogen. A solid rocket booster is on each side.

STATS & FACTS

LAUNCHED: 1981

ORIGIN: US

MODELS: *DISCOVERY, ATLANTIS, ENDEAVOUR, COLOMBIA, CHALLENGER*

ENGINES: THREE ORBITER ENGINES THAT EACH PRODUCE A VACUUM THRUST OF 213,188 KG

WINGSPAN: 23.79 M

LENGTH: 37.24 M

CREW: UP TO 10

MAXIMUM SPEED: 28,164 KM/H (17,500 MPH)

MAXIMUM LANDING WEIGHT: 100 TONNES

RANGE: 187-643 KM (116-403 MILES)

LOAD: SATELLITES, COMPONENTS FOR THE JOINT SPACE STATION AND SPACE EXPERIMENTS

COST: £1.05 BILLION, PLUS £278 MILLION FOR EACH LAUNCH

On December 23, 1986, a strange looking aircraft landed at Edwards Air Force Base, California. It had taken off from the same runway nine days before and flown nonstop around the world. This had never been done before.

Voyager was made of carbon fibre and glass fibre. At rest, its wings scraped the ground, but in flight they curved upward like the wings of a bird.

DID YOU KNOW?

During its epic journey, *Voyager* covered 40,211 km (24,986 miles).

Voyager is on display in the Smithsonian Institution's National Air and Space Museum alongside other famous aircraft such as the *Wright Flyer* and Charles Lindbergh's *Spirit of St. Louis*.

Voyager was one of many unusual aircrafts created by Bert Rutan. His brother Dick and Jeana Yeager flew the plane.

STATS & FACTS

LAUNCHED: 1985

RETIRED: 1987

ORIGIN: US

MODELS: ONE

ENGINES: TWO TELEDYNE CONTINENTAL ENGINES (FRONT 130 BHP, REAR 110 BHP)

WINGSPAN: 33.8 M

LENGTH: 8.9 M

COCKPIT CREW: TWO

MAXIMUM SPEED: 196 KM/H (122 MPH)

MAXIMUM WEIGHT: 4.4 TONNES

RANGE: 44,185 KM (27,475 MILES)

LOAD: TWO CREW MEMBERS

COST: £618,400

X-43A

NASA (National Aeronautics and Space Administration) is best known for space exploration, but it also conducts important research into aircraft. The X-43A is one of the latest research planes. It is a hypersonic (faster than Mach 5) plane that flies without a pilot.

Guinness World Records recognised the X-43A Scramjet with a world speed record for a jet-powered aircraft – an amazing Mach 9.6!

DID YOU KNOW?

At high Mach speeds the heat is so great that metal portions of the plane's frame melt.

The X-43A's first flight took place on 2nd June 2001. It was dropped from a B-52 over the Pacific Ocean. However, the plane broke up in the sky.

The X-43A has a wide bottom, flat top and two fins. Its Scramjet engine burns hydrogen-based fuel.

STATS & FACTS

LAUNCHED: 2001 (TEST VERSION)

ORIGIN: US

MODELS: X-43A, X-43B, X-43C, X-43D

ENGINE: GASL HYDROGEN-FUELLED SCRAMJET ENGINE

WINGSPAN: 1.5 M

LENGTH: 3.66 M

CREW: UNMANNED AT PRESENT

MAXIMUM SPEED: MACH 10 (10,622 KM/H / 6,600 MPH)

MAXIMUM WEIGHT: 1.3 TONNES

RANGE: UNKNOWN

COST: £150 MILLION

AFTERBURNER System that injects extra fuel into the exhaust gases of a plane to provide large amounts of extra power.

AIR REFUELLING Method of refuelling military aircraft while in flight, via a fuel hose linked to a tanker aircraft.

BOOSTERS Large canisters containing fuel that are attached to the sides of a space rocket as it is launched.

CABIN The enclosed space in an aircraft or spacecraft that holds the crew, passengers and cargo.

CARBON/GLASS FIBRE A modern strong, but lightweight material.

COCKPIT The part of an aircraft where the pilot and his assistants sit.

EJECTION SEAT A seat, usually installed in military aircraft, that can be fired or ejected from the aircraft.

ENGINE The part of a plane where fuel is burned to create energy.

EXHAUSTS Pipes at the back of a plane that let out poisonous gases made when fuel is burned.

FOREPLANES Moveable surfaces at the front of a plane that provide extra lift and balance.

FREIGHTER An aircraft made to carry cargo rather than passengers.

FUSELAGE See Cabin.

HOLD The lower part of a plane where cargo is stored.

HYPERSONIC Able to reach speeds of Mach 5 and above.

JETS Part of an engine that provides the lifting power for an aircraft.

LASER GUIDED BOMB A bomb launched from an aircraft that has sensors in its nose to guide it onto a target.

MACH Measurement that relates the speed of an aircraft to the speed of sound. Mach 1 is the speed of sound; Mach 2 is twice the speed of sound.

NOSE The rounded front of an aircraft.

ORBITER A spacecraft or satellite designed to orbit a planet or other body without landing on it.

PARACHUTE A large canopy with a body harness underneath. It is designed to slow the rate of descent of a person from an aircraft.

PILOT A person qualified to fly an aircraft or spaceship.

PROPELLER A machine with spinning blades that provides thrust to lift an aircraft.

RADAR A method of detecting distant objects using radio waves.

SCRAMJET A hydrogen-fuelled engine designed for flying at five times the speed of sound.

SENSORS Devices that help pilots fly their aircraft, detect enemy aircraft or fire weapons accurately.

STEALTH TECHNOLOGY Technology used to make a plane almost invisible.

SUPERSONIC Faster than the speed of sound.

SUBSONIC Slower than the speed of sound.

TAIL The rear part of the fuselage that balances a plane.

THRUST A pushing force created in a jet engine or rocket that gives aircraft enough speed to take off.

TITANIUM ALLOY A light, strong and heat-tolerant material.

TURBOFAN An engine with a fan used to boost its power.

TURBINE Machine with a wheel or rotor driven by water, steam or gases.

VTOL Vertical Take-off, Vertical Landing. System that holds an aircraft in the air as it takes off or lands.

VIFF Vectoring in Forward Flight. A system that lets a plane change direction very suddenly.

WINGSPAN The distance between the tips of the wings of an aircraft.

WINGS Part of the aircraft that provides lift, placed on each side of the fuselage.